WOMEN LOVING WOMEN

JAMYE WAXMAN

"SEX ED" COLUMNIST
FOR *PLAYGIRL* MAGAZINE

WOMEN LOVING WOMEN

APPRECIATING AND EXPLORING THE BEAUTY
OF EROTIC FEMALE ENCOUNTERS

QUIVER

Text © 2007 Quiver
Photography © 2007 Rockport Publishers

First published in the USA in 2007 by
Quiver, a member of
Quayside Publishing Group
33 Commercial Street
Gloucester, MA 01930
www.quiverbooks.com

11 10 09 08 07   1 2 3 4 5

ISBN-13: 978-1-59233-258-8
ISBN-10: 1-59233-258-7

Library of Congress Cataloging-in-Publication Data available

Cover and book design by Carol Holtz
Book production by Rachel Fitzgibbon
Photography by Allan Penn Photography

Printed and bound in Singapore

DEDICATION

To all the women who have shared their strories or have been part of mine.

CONTENTS

INTRODUCTION 8

1
CLOSE ENCOUNTERS
OF THE SAME KIND 14
LIKE ATTRACTS LIKE 16
ASKING "Y" 28

2
SCENT OF A WOMAN 34
TOUCH 37
SMELL 42
TASTE 44

3
IN THE BEGINNING 48
STARTING WITH ONE 50
MAPPING IT OUT 54
FOR THE VERY FIRST TIME 62

4
KNOW THYSELF 66
ANATOMICALLY SPEAKING 68
TALK DIRTY TO ME 80

5
SPEAKING IN TONGUES 82
OPEN UP AND SAY "AAAAH" 84
THE TONGUE IS MIGHTIER THAN 86
    THE SWORD
ASSUMING THE POSITION 92

6
TOY STORIES 96
WHY WE LOVE TOYS 98
THE VIBRATIONAL PULL 100
SHOP GIRL 105

7
THREE'S COMPANY 106
THREE IS NOT A CROWD 108
THREE-WAYS: TIPS AND 110
    TECHNIQUES TO SHOW
    YOU THE WAY
POTENTIAL MÉNAGE À TROIS 112
    MISTAKES

8
THE MAGIC GARDEN 114
A STATE OF MIND 116
ON A LARGER SCALE 119
WOMEN ARE BEAUTIFUL 121

9
OH THE PLACES
YOU'LL GO 122
PLACES TO MEET 124
COME TO SHOP OR SHOP 124
    TO COME
VIDEOS 125

ACKNOWLEDGMENTS 127
ABOUT THE AUTHOR 127

INTRODUCTION

HOME SWEET HOME

Women loving women is a concept that has been around since the dawn of humanity. It's about the simple attraction of like to like. People, in general, like to surround themselves with the things they're accustomed to—we often live in an area similar to the one in which we grew up, we tend to hang out with groups of people with similar interests (people who might look like us, act like us, and possibly even think like us), we remain close to our families, and some of us stay tight with our best friends from childhood. Some of us create new families for ourselves as we discover who we truly want to be.

Whether we recreate or reinterpret what home is, there really is no place like it. Even if we aren't back at the home of our past, the home of our present is where we feel safe and secure. If we look at the physical house as the place where we live, we can also look at our bodies as another type of home. Our bodies are our temples, the transportable and beautiful sanctuaries that house our souls, our thoughts, and our desires. Our bodies are our homes, and they are sacred.

If you've ever thought about a sexual homecoming, *Women Loving Women* is a perfect way to find your way home. Deciding to love another woman is like deciding to find a new way to love yourself. After all, women are not all that different from one another, no matter if we look, act, or feel as if we are.

"*I like everything. Boyish girls, girlish boys, the heavy, and the skinny. Which is a problem when I'm walking down the street.*"

–Angelina Jolie,
actress

As women, we have certain feminine qualities, such as our hips, our breasts, and our vulvas. As women, we can relate to other women, because we share those physical attributes, as well as a similar mental and emotional state of being. If you stop and think about how many times you've talked with your girlfriend about how hard it is to communicate with your man, and she understands and says something back such as, "Why doesn't he just do A or B?" you know what I mean.

Loving a woman teaches us about ourselves, our bodies, and our own emotions. It teaches us that there truly is no place like home, and that sometimes it feels nice to go back there. Loving another woman is, in a sense, returning home.

We are constantly evolving, experiencing, and exploring. In life and in love, we are continually learning about the type of people we are and the situations we'd like to explore. Sexuality is fluid, and therefore, as we continue to grow and change, so do our sexual preferences. Sometimes it's just about the positions we screw in, and other times it's about the relationships we form. Regardless of the path we take, if we don't satisfy our curiosity, we often live with regret. If you have picked up this book, you are at least curious, and I am here to give you permission to not only read on but to sexplore.

Now I'll make a personal confession. I've had same-sex experiences for as long as I've been sexual, and I know that having them isn't always easy to accept. It took me years to understand and be comfortable with the course of my actions. This was all before it was cool to play the field and "bat for your own team." And now, as I grow up and explore my own self, I've learned that I am open and accepting of all sexualities, and that I can acknowledge and enjoy more than one type of sex. It feels good to be open to experiment. The question remains: How open are you?

1
CLOSE ENCOUNTERS OF
THE SAME KIND

LIKE ATTRACTS LIKE

Women are beautiful, sensual beings. We are soft, fleshy, tender, thick, thin, juicy, sweet, sour, curvaceous, and voluptuous. We are listeners, nurturers, doctors, peacemakers, and providers. We are leaders and followers. Our lives have at least a dash of both sugar and spice, and we can be naughty or polite, daring or demure, self-sacrificing or self-seeking. We are the stronger sex, if not physically than mentally. We are feminine, we are masculine, and we are continually redefining what it means to be a woman. Everybody loves us, even if they aren't in love with us. We are admired for our beauty and our shape. We are attractive—not only to men, but also to other women. And this is why we do what we do.

This is why we do what we do. We apply makeup, get dressed up, and present our beautiful selves to the rest of the world. We don't necessarily do these things for the men in our lives, but instead for the women we will encounter as we go about our daily business. Women do things for other women because often it's these other women that notice what we do and who we are. When a woman wakes up in the morning, how often do you think she is dressing for a man? Not all that often. When we put on our "face" in the morning, is it more for the men in our lives, or the women we will brush past over the course of our day? From whom do we need to stand out? The answer is other women.

We're always competing with the more enticing and attractive of the sexes. Men admire women simply because we are more attractive, but women appreciate women for how they appear. We admire other women, and we want them to admire us too. And quite often, there is some underlying attraction.

"I love the way a woman feels. A woman has a softness and tenderness about her that you can't feel in a man. And all women feel soft and tender, even though it can be in different places. Finding those soft spots is part of uncovering the beauty of woman."

—Sara, 39

" Do I like women sexually?

Yeah, I do."

—Drew Barrymore, actress

ALTHOUGH IT'S MORE ACCEPTABLE
AND TALKED ABOUT TODAY, SAME-
SEX EXPERIENCES BETWEEN
HETEROSEXUAL WOMEN HAVE BEEN
GOING ON THROUGHOUT HISTORY.

Saint Joan of Arc

(January 6, 1412–May 30, 1431)
There's much controversy surrounding
the sexuality of Saint Joan of Arc, the
peasant girl turned national heroine
of France. According to a biography by
Vita Sackville-West (the same woman
who had a "*women-loving-women*"
affair with Virginia Woolf), Joan of
Arc definitely had a love for females,
and possibly a few dalliances with
other young women. St. Joan often
dressed in men's clothes and shared
her bed with younger women. Other
historians argue that this is just a sign
of the times, and that nothing can be
deduced from Sackville-West's study.
But nobody knows for sure. Did Joan
of Arc love other women? Anything
is possible.

It's not a bad or scary thing to find another woman attractive. In fact, it's totally normal. *Like attracts like.* It's something science taught us at a young age. It's something that's been instilled in our brains. It's something we understand before we ever truly explored what it means. Same-sex attraction is only natural. It's a part of who we are.

We love things with which we are familiar. The smell of our clothing, the scent of our familial home, and the comfort of being around the people we care about. These are the things that make us feel calm and relaxed. That's why it's easy to find ourselves attracted to our best friend, our coworker, our teacher, or a random stranger who's got that certain something. *Like attracts like.* Sexuality proves this fact again and again.

" *I was excited by images of females before I had any sexual interest in men, but at the time it was somewhat subconscious and didn't freak me out. The first 'real' girl I liked was a high school friend. We were oh, so coffee-house alterna-cool that we thought it would be fun and quirky to kiss each other hello and goodbye on the mouth. Just pecks—it was never more than that; I didn't think she meant it as any more than that, but I enjoyed it. I definitely had a big crush on her.*"

—Kiley, 27

Have you ever had a same-sex attraction? If you're reading this, odds are you have. Maybe you've thought about what it might be like to brush your lips against another woman's soft belly. Think about the first time you thought about what another woman might feel like. Was it your first roommate, or someone you met one summer on holiday? Remember, attraction doesn't mean you've necessarily acted out your fantasy, or that you've even told anybody else about it, but it does mean that you've got the itch, some sort of curious desire to know more. And while you never have to act out your fantasy, what's the harm in trying?

"The realization that I was attracted to other women was rather subtle. I would always check out the other girls in the locker room while changing after cheerleading or basketball, really just to compare our bodies. Eventually, I would start to kiss my girlfriends during games of truth-or-dare, really to entice the guys, but it wasn't supposed to be sexual. In fact, I never had an actual sexual experience with another girl during high school. Now that's changed in college, especially since I learned that this was my time for total sexual freedom. And what a time it's been!"

—Mariah, 19

" Different though the sexes are, they intermix. In every human being a vacillation from one sex to the other takes place, and often it is only the clothes that keep the male or female likeness, while underneath the sex is the very opposite of what it is above."

—Virginia Woolf, author

ALTHOUGH IT'S MORE ACCEPTABLE
AND TALKED ABOUT TODAY, SAME-
SEX EXPERIENCES BETWEEN
HETEROSEXUAL WOMEN HAVE BEEN
GOING ON THROUGHOUT HISTORY.

Virginia Woolf

(January 25, 1882–March 28, 1941)
Author, essayist, critic, feminist, and
central figure in the Bloomsbury Group,
Virginia Stephen married the writer
and critic Leonard Woolf in 1912.
Together they founded Hogarth Press,
publishing the works of ground-
breakers, such as the poet T. S. Eliot and
the Austrian-born "father of psycho-
analysis," Sigmund Freud. Although
Woolf was married, it was in 1922 that
she began a romantic relationship with
poet and novelist Vita Sackville-West.
Their affair lasted throughout most
of the 1920s and the two remained
friends even after their relationship
ended (up until Woolf's suicide in
1941). It is said that Sackville-West
had a significant effect on Woolf, with
many believing Woolf wrote and published her 1928 boundary-breaking
novel *Orlando* as a result of their
mutual love.

Why are modern-day women more likely to talk about, and encourage others to try, same-sex encounters? For starters, sex is everywhere. From billboards to fashion magazines and on TV, you can't turn around without hearing a discussion about sex. Newsmakers are also getting in on the game. They're talking about their same-sex experiences, and accepting them for what they are. Ellen DeGeneres and Anne Heche are not only two powerful women in Hollywood, they were also, for a time, one of the most well-known Hollywood couples. Women warmed up to Ellen for coming out. Women wondered about Anne for being open to sexual exploration. But what's there to wonder about? Sexuality is constantly morphing. It is continually changing, whether or not we decide to go with the flow. We can fight it, ignore it, or explore it. It's our choice to make.

"We do not fall in love with the package of the person, we fall in love with the inside of a person."

—Anne Heche, actress

Emily Dickinson

(December 10, 1830–May 15, 1886)
While poet Emily Dickinson was often thought to have had a male mentor, whom she sometimes referred to as "Master," throughout a significant portion of her life, she actually corresponded with a woman named Susan Gilbert. Gilbert was her eventual sister-in-law, extremely close friend, and possibly her lover. While some scholars believe the relationship was strictly platonic, Dickinson's relations with Gilbert, as discovered through their postal correspondence, were obviously more involved than that. Although it was defined as a "romantic friendship," the letters Dickinson wrote to Gilbert were often erotic in nature, signifying a rather strong female bond. Gilbert's family destroyed all the correspondence upon her death, but Dickinson's letters were published in 1998 in a collection titled *Open Me Carefully.*

ALTHOUGH IT'S MORE ACCEPTABLE
AND TALKED ABOUT TODAY, SAME-
SEX EXPERIENCES BETWEEN
HETEROSEXUAL WOMEN HAVE BEEN
GOING ON THROUGHOUT HISTORY.

Eleanor Roosevelt

(October 11, 1884–November 7, 1962)
Eleanor Roosevelt was arguably one of the
most powerful women of her time. As the
niece of one president, the wife of another,
an author, a speaker, and a political figure,
Roosevelt was a well-known and central
figure in U.S. history. She had it all—success,
fame, power, respect, and money. What many
didn't know, however, was that Roosevelt also
had a female lover, Associated Press reporter
Lorena Hickok. They became close friends in
1932, and stayed friends until Roosevelt's
death in 1962. At one point Hickok even lived
in the White House with the Roosevelts. While
not all of her family agrees that their relationship was more than platonic, a book of
private correspondence, *Empty Without You:
The Intimate Letters of Eleanor Roosevelt
and Lorena Hickok*, was published in 1998,
adding credence to the claim that a strong
romantic bond existed between the two.

Society has given women permission to experiment. We've been told experimenting won't make us gay, unless of course we choose to be gay, which is part of the discovery process. We've been encouraged to openly experiment in a natural and carefree sort of way. Not everybody who has had a same-sex encounter is willing to share her experiences, but many are, and therefore it's easy to find the information you need to never feel alone in what you're doing. Plus, it's fun, and supersexy. There's nothing like rediscovering your own self through the body of another, and it seems as if almost everyone has done it. The Internet lets us find chat rooms that tell us we're not alone. It's acceptable because sex is out there and because it's something new to try.

" *My first real girl kiss was in college, dancing at the local watering hole, when a very hot older classmate named Casey just reeled me in and kissed me while her boyfriend, Matt, looked on. And that was that. It felt like an initiation, a baptism into experimenting with other women.* "

—Annie, 31

ASKING "Y"

Why are there so few recorded relationships between two women? Odds are that because society doesn't discuss, or accept, lots of things regarding sex, the only relationships recorded and acknowledged have had to involve a pair of Xs along with an XY. However, the times, they are a-changing!

Nowadays, it's cool to be a LUG (lesbian until graduation) and to share your same-sex experiences with your friends. It's even acceptable to change your sexuality from one day to the next. I've had friends who were staunch dykes, never even looking sexually at a man, and now they are engaged to be married to a guy in the traditional sort of way, to the traditional type of person. I've had female friends who've only been in relationships with men and are just now living their lives with female companions. As long as you stay open to progress, it's cool to evolve. And it's not as if you can't go back. And forth. And back. And forth.

"Don't compromise yourself. You are all you've got."
—Janis Joplin,
singer/songwriter

Janis Joplin

(January 19, 1943–October 4, 1970) Singer and songwriter Janis Joplin certainly had a distinctive lifestyle to go along with her distinctive voice. She came into her sexuality during the revolutionary "hippie" days of San Francisco's Haight-Ashbury era. A talented musician, Joplin never cared much about labeling her sexuality, and she refused to call herself straight, gay, or bi. While she dated men, such as Kris Kristofferson and Country Joe McDonald, she also loved women, and it was rumored that at one time she had a relationship with the musician Janis Ian.

We often have an epiphany at some point in our lives. We ask ourselves why we are who we are, and why we like who we like. We examine our relationships, both within the context of self and with the people we care about. We may realize that we don't have a type of person we relate to, or we realize that we do, but we also recognize that certain things, certain tastes change over time. We might even let our inquisitiveness get the best of us, and that's when we become curious enough to act out our discoveries. Or we might not. We might secretly just fantasize about our deepest, darkest desires or we might rent a video depicting what we want to see, just so we get to watch. We might even take things a step further. If, at some point, we decide to act on something new that turns us on, then we have to find ways to accept it. If we can own it and not be embarrassed by it, we have nothing to hide. And that's the best feeling in the world. So, instead of asking "why?," ask "why not?"

I've always lived by the quote "I'd rather regret something I did than something I didn't do," because life should not be about asking questions without seeking answers. Today we understand more about the relationships between sex, gender, and aging. We've had people such as Masters and Johnson, Sheri Hite, and Alfred Kinsey willing to scientifically study sex. We continue to learn more about the way sexuality, and female sexuality in particular, evolves, because of women such as Candida Royalle, Nancy Friday, and Annie Sprinkle. And we can only continue to learn and to grow.

" *In America, sex is an obsession; in other parts of the world, it's a fact.*"

—Marlene Dietrich,
actress and singer

X WITHOUT Y

"I'd kiss a girl again. The Madonna thing was a one-off, but girls are nice to kiss—nice and soft."

—Christina Aguilera, singer

Men are beautiful creatures, and by no means is anybody saying that men aren't fun or sexy, or good in bed; it's just that women can provide a nourishing quality and nurturing encounter that you can't necessarily have with a man. It's something instinctual, something maternal—something innate.

Enjoying women isn't about hating men, or leaving your man, or never loving another man again. It's about bonding—female bonding—and about forming ties with other women. It's about the secret society of sisterhood and unique friendships—friendships based on a mutual love, admiration, trust, and respect. It's about giving yourself permission to explore and to experience something that you can't feel with a man. It's about the experience of getting to know your own body through the lens of another woman's gaze.

Such an experience can be taught only by someone who shares the same inner workings as you do, someone who can understand what it means to menstruate, to grow breasts, to birth a child. It's not like the balance a man can provide, it's more like the education a woman can give. It's unique. It's exciting. And it's something worth trying. Even if it's just once in this lifetime.

"It's not that I don't like men, not at all; I like them a lot. It's just that women offer a different experience. They're soft and they smell sweet. Their skin is fun to touch, and for me, being with a woman allows me to really explore my gentle side."

—Christa, 29

2

SCENT OF
A WOMAN

TOUCH

We are born with the desire to be touched. It's called skin hunger, and it's something that is ingrained in us as soon as we enter this world. Skin hunger is satisfied through touch, and it's one of the most important forms of trust, caring, and communication two people can experience. If babies aren't touched enough, they cry; if adults aren't touched enough, they retreat into a solitary space. It's because we need touch.

Skin-to-skin contact is a way for us to express certain feelings without ever having to communicate through spoken language. Touch is a silent language. For example, a reassuring hug sends the message that everything is okay. A soft, delicate brush of one's hand down another person's arm can signal a longing or arousal. A gentle massage can make a person go weak in the knees, while a pat on the butt can send us into playful submission.

It's important to maintain touch with anyone with whom you connect, but how often do you actually think about what it is you're touching? How often do you let your mind register every small detail of another person's body? How often do you stop and think how it feels to be with a man? How often do you stop and think how it feels, or will feel, to be with a woman? Take a moment to stop and imagine.

TEN WAYS
TO SATISFY
SKIN HUNGER:
1. MASSAGE
2. SPANKING
3. HUGGING
4. MASTURBATING
5. INTERCOURSE
6. RUBBING
7. BITING
8. HOLDING HANDS
9. SCRATCHING
10. CUDDLING

"*A woman is like a tea bag; you never know how strong she is until she gets into hot water.*"

—Eleanor Roosevelt

" *When I first feel her vagina, I start*
to lose control. It's like unwrapping
a gift. You don't know what you're
going to uncover, until you slowly
peel back the folds, and then, and
only then, can you actually feel her.
I mean feel what's inside her. How
cool is that?!"

—Virginia, 24

WOMEN'S FEELINGS

"I love how another woman feels. I adore the softness of skin, where the ear meets the neck, long hair . . . everything!"

—Virginia, 24

A woman is smooth, like a baby's bottom, especially in certain soft and meaty spots. The inner bits of her thighs and where the mound meets the flesh are among the silkiest and most delicate of places. A woman has tender, fleshy bits around her belly and thighs. Her breasts are meant to be cupped and caressed, regardless of whether they are large and full, small and rounded, or anywhere in between. Her nipples may feel like a colony of tiny bumps or a smooth lunar surface. They may be small and dark or large and pale, but no matter what, you should brush your hands over them, because they feel nice. A woman is curved around the hips and she is tighter around the waist. Run your hands down her sides and feel her silhouette. Of course, there are also her genitals, the mound of flesh that forms a triangle at the top of her thighs. You should touch her above the mound and below the belly button to send a tingly sensation inside her vulva. You should touch her lips, her clitoris, and the insides of her folds. Each woman will feel different, which is the beauty of being uniquely female. We feel different on the outside *and* the inside.

"When I'm first being touched, I like it to start out slow. Gentle. Not fast and hard, no vigorous hand movements. You can start by just barely running your fingers over my breasts, and spend a little time playing with my belly. Tease me. Don't go to my genitals before you go to my feet. Start at the top and work your way to the bottom. Then work your way back. No matter what you do, just make sure to touch me, to touch me a lot."

—Jessica, 39

You are woman, and you have a million tiny crevices that cry out for attention. There are so many great places to touch on your body, so go ahead and touch them all. See how it feels to run your fingers up and down your neck, to gently glide the tips of your nails in the space between your breasts. Rub your belly and squeeze on the tummy you spend hours trying to shrink away. Tickle the inner part of your arms and massage between your toes. Using your hands, gently touch yourself in a circular motion on the innermost parts of your thighs. Spend a moment touching the back of your knee, and another minute tenderly flicking the lobe of your ear. Massage below the belly button, above the pubic mound. Have someone else touch these spots for you. What does it do for you? Does it turn you on?

"My favorite part of a woman's body is her torso, just under her breasts, that smooth line down her belly toward her hips, and that little V shape that leads from there toward her pubic area. Wow! Don't get me wrong; I still appreciate a man's body, and am very attracted to men in general, but something about being a woman, and being with a woman, just seems right."

—Mary, 28

APPLYING A MASSAGE-LIKE PRESSURE RIGHT ABOVE THE PUBIC MOUND, A FEW INCHES BELOW HER BELLY BUTTON, WILL HELP INCREASE HER SEXUAL SENSIBILITY. SHE'LL BE MORE AWARE OF HER SEXUAL ENERGY, WHICH, IN TURN, WILL GET HER MORE AROUSED.

There are many forms of touch that a woman might like to feel, from the subtle to the obvious. There's rubbing, sucking, scratching, biting, and then there's spanking, caning, and flogging. There isn't any one way to touch somebody, but the best way to start is by placing your hands on some part of her body. Connect through skin-to-skin contact and then decide what other forms of contact you might like to try. No matter what touch you like, touch you must.

FLOGGING AND CANING ARE PART OF IMPACT PLAY. IN FLOGGING, ONE PERSON IS STRUCK WITH A FLEXIBLE OBJECT, USUALLY A FLOGGER, WHICH CONSISTS OF A HANDLE AND A LEATHER OR RUBBER TAIL. CANING INVOLVES THE USE OF A CANE, A LONG, STRAIGHT WOODEN STICK GENERALLY MADE OF BAMBOO. BEGINNERS SHOULD STICK TO STRIKING THE RECEIVER ON THE BUTTOCKS.

SMELL

"Women perceive odors better than men do. A woman's smell can release a host of memories. So the right human smell at the right moment could touch off vivid pleasant memories and possibly ignite that first, stunning moment of romantic adoration."

—Helen Fisher, author and research professor of anthropology

From her pits to her toes, what is the scent of a woman? Is it rose petals floating on a bed of water? Is it the scent of lavender or the cool smell of cucumber? Is it more musky, or even a little tart? Maybe she smells like your favorite detergent, bar of soap, or body lotion. Whatever it is, the scent of a woman will vary, not only from person to person but also from day to day. For starters, let's get over the negative things that we think about when we think of how a woman smells. Because the truth of it is that a healthy woman smells fragrant and beautiful, no matter if she smells like lemons or lavender. How she smells is part of her body's natural chemistry, and how you smell her is part of the overall enjoyment of the female experience.

Oftentimes we think it's the physical sight of a person that allows us to experience the tender emotions of love. But the truth is that the strongest "scent-sual" attraction comes from our noses. According to the Smell and Taste Treatment and Research Center, our sense of smell is what keeps us attracted to our lover. Technically speaking, the associations between smell and emotion happen because our olfactory receptors are directly connected to the part of our brain known as the limbic system, commonly referred to as the brain's pleasure center. Not so technically, the scent of a person brings up certain memories and emotions that help us maintain an attraction to him or her.

"Pussy has a divine natural fragrance that shouldn't be washed away or masked with deodorant spray. The smell of a woman's arousal is intoxicating. If someone could find a way to bottle the scent of a woman, I'd buy it and splash some on every day. Right after my shower even."

—Lippy Imp, writer, blogger, book reviewer

Women have their own special odor, and most people would agree that as long as it's not overwhelming, it's extremely sexy. According to a study at the University of Texas, Austin, women smell sexiest when they are their most fertile. What this means is that the scent of a woman changes with her cycle. Even if it's not fertility that drives you wild, one thing is certain: We all emit pheromones, a mixture of chemicals released through our sweat glands. While they aren't something we can consciously recognize, they are unconsciously what attracts us to certain people. Since we all have our own smell, one that's unique to each and every one of us, we emit our own signal that reaches and affects every person individually. That's why we're attracted to one person and not to another. The more positive the emotional effect of a smell, the more attracted we'll be to the person behind the scent. Beauty isn't just in the eye of the beholder, it's really the nose that knows.

TASTE

Unfortunately, society gives a woman's taste a pretty bad rap. From obnoxious fish jokes to douches and other personal hygiene systems, women are told that how they naturally smell and taste is totally unnatural. We often forget that the vagina is a self-cleaning oven, and that when a woman's not being affected by outside elements (such as infection), things take care of themselves quite nicely. It stinks that women have had to defend the smell of their vulvas, because natural scent is a total turn-on for lots of women, and for lots of men, too. For most people who appreciate the taste of a woman, what they expect before they go down and what they actually experience never match up. You can't tell how a woman will taste by how she looks, but generally, the taste of a woman is pleasant and delicious.

So what does a woman taste like? It can be an array of flavors, ranging from the sweet to sour, to bitter, tart, or slightly metallic. Women can also taste salty, buttery, and lemony; it all depends on who it is you're tasting and how she tastes on that particular day. How do you taste? If you're not sure, then what are you waiting for? It's important to taste yourself and get connected with your own bodily juices. Go ahead; slide a finger in there and taste for yourself.

How a woman tastes depends on her hormone balance and body chemistry. It's important to remember that every cell of our bodies is affected by the acid/alkaline measurement, or the pH level, of our internal fluids. The perfect pH for our body is 6.4 (though our skin's pH tends to range anywhere between 6.0 and 7.0). Anything above that means our bodies are more alkaline, while anything below that means our bodies are more acidic. As for a woman's vulva, which is much more acidic than her skin, a healthy pH can vary anywhere from 4.1 to 5.0.

So what does this all mean? It means that there's more than some truth to the phrase "You are what you eat." If, for example, a woman takes vitamins, eats lots of garlic, and drinks lots of alcohol, this can all have a negative impact on her taste. If she eats parsley or mint, or drinks certain less acidic juices (such as pear or carrot juice), she might taste slightly sweet.

"Aging affects the consistency and availability of vaginal lubrications; between puberty and menopause, women have more secretions. And the more stress a woman has, the more pungent she may become. Pungency can be affected by her natural body chemistry, her diet, and any meds she takes, including over-the-counter ones. Since smell and taste are so closely related, a woman who shaves or trims her pubic hair may have less of a scent than a woman with a dank bush— giving the illusion that she has less of a taste."

—Dr. Carol Queen, author,
sex educator, activist

Because how one smells and how one tastes can vary, it's important to stay in communication with your partner if, at some point, something smells or tastes off. Usually when someone's taste is unbearable, it means that something else, such as an infection, is going on. If that's the case, suggest that your lover see a doctor to take care of any impending problems.

" Since I first experimented with Lisa, I can't get enough of the taste of her box. Sometimes I even fantasize when I'm at work about how she tastes. While I still enjoy the taste of a man, being with a woman has awakened a new sense within me."

—Tina, 35

"My love for women is a deep, inherent, and primal thing. The fancier and femmier the woman is, the more I have a chemical reaction to attraction. There is no theory or thought . . . I swoon in the presence of a woman offering herself to me and pleading for her orgasm, especially when the woman in focus smells good, tastes good, has good hygiene, doesn't smoke, doesn't do drugs, is fierce and confidently sexy."

—Jackie Strano, producer, director

It's hot to taste your partner, and taste extends beyond that of our juicy, luscious vulvas. How a partner's skin tastes can also be a major turn-on, and for the partner getting tasted, it's definitely going to be pleasurable. The skin is an erogenous zone, and there's lots of territory to cover. Skin can taste salty, or it can have a slight, almost undetectable flavor. It all depends on the spaces and places being tasted. When making love to a woman, it's important to taste the rest of her body as well.

We all have certain preferences for the tastes we like and the ones we don't like. Compare it to when we go to a restaurant and look at the menu: There are certain flavors and types of foods that turn us on, and others that turn us off. If you are with a partner and aren't into the taste, talk to her about it. Maybe it has something to do with her diet. Maybe it has something to do with her hygiene. Find ways to help adjust your discomfort. Adding things that sweeten a diet, such as parsley or mint, can also sweeten the taste. Reducing things such as meat, alcohol, and tobacco can do a lot for reducing bitterness. It's not that you should have to change the taste of a lover, because a woman should taste finger-licking good just the way she is, but the taste of a woman shouldn't limit what you're willing to do. Once you get past certain issues, you'll be able to delight in the touch, scent, and taste of a woman.

3

IN THE
BEGINNING

STARTING WITH ONE

Maybe you've already been with a woman and the experience was less than stellar. Maybe you've thought about doing it but then decided to skip the opportunity when it knocked on your door. Perhaps you think you're passed experimenting and don't know what you could possibly get out of some female-to-female companionship. Or maybe you've never really thought much about it before, but now the thought keeps crossing your mind. Whatever the case, remember that sexuality is fluid and that we are constantly growing. That's why it often happens that as we embrace who we are, we also start to think outside of the box. Or maybe we just think more about box. Whatever the case, there may be some form of box involved.

Perhaps being with another woman was a fantasy we had in college, but now we feel well past our glory days. Or maybe we get off thinking about women, but it's never been a something we've acted on. The truth is we can be and can do whatever we want; it's just a matter of how badly we want to do it.

" The first time I was with a woman, it was because she plopped herself down on my lap and started making out with me. I decided to take it further, so I led her to the guest bedroom and figured out what to do. Turns out it was her first time with a girl, too. It was awesome. I liked being bigger than her, being in control, which was never the case with me with guys. It didn't feel weird at all. It felt totally natural."

—Heather, 27

" The first time I thought about being with a woman, I was too young to really understand what it all meant. I thought that finding my neighbor attractive was normal, only she wasn't too keen on the idea. It was weird at first, because I wanted to explore things sexually, and she wasn't into it. Years later, when I ran into her after college, it turned out she was dating another woman. I guess I had brought up some feelings that she wasn't ready to deal with. I, on the other hand, wasn't waiting around, and within a few weeks I had found another girl who wanted to play."

—Theresa, 29

Having same-sex feelings isn't always easy to deal with. Maybe you have some guilt about how you feel, or perhaps you go as far as thinking that your thoughts are dirty and shameful. What's really important to remember is that you are not alone. These ideas are nothing to be ashamed of, and lots of women have thought about being with another woman. Lots of women have acted out their fantasies. Currently there are whole groups of young women who have referred or do refer to themselves as LUGs (lesbians until graduation). Both men's and women's magazines are constantly writing about this supposed "trend" and talking with women who like to experiment with other women.

But it's not a trend. It's been happening since people have been having sex, only now it's both socially acceptable and hip. Sometimes it seems as if everybody's doing it. Society has become more socially tolerant of women loving women. While not all of us can grasp the idea of dueling swords that don't always duel, we've become quite accustomed to, and sometimes turned on by, the idea of two women getting it on. I'm not one who's big on double standards, but I can definitely see why the idea of two young, soft, fleshy, and pink personalities appeals to a larger, more mainstream audience. Sex with another woman can be an intense, beautiful, and romantic reality. It can also be awkward, funny, and complicated. There are lots of things it can be, but the one thing it is, no matter how it turns out, is a growing and learning experience.

MAPPING IT OUT

Before delving into the beautiful world of all that is female, it's best to make sure you know your own body. Do you know the places you like to be touched, and just how you like it to feel? Do you enjoy a soft touch? Or do you prefer your partner to apply a bit more pressure? Do you fancy circular movements instead of strokes, or do you like her to rub up and down, rather than from side to side? Knowing what you like will help you get the most of what you want.

So let's take a look at a woman's body. While her brain is her most powerful sex organ (and his, too!), she has ears, a neck, and a collarbone where her neck meets her shoulders. There are breasts, and places under the breasts, and nipples and belly buttons, and the happy trail that leads from her belly to her mound. There are fingers and toes and buttocks, and the place right above the butt where some women have a small patch of hair. There are scalps and foreheads and lots of other little places just waiting to be discovered. And then, of course, there's the vulva.

VOLUPTUOUS VULVA

The vulva refers to all the external bits of a woman's genitals. Those bits include her outer lips and her mound. Other parts of her nethers include her inner lips, her clitoris, her vagina, her fourchette (the fold of skin that forms the posterior margin of the vulva), perineum, and anus, as well as a myriad of other local hot spots to stop in and visit.

" I love to worship a woman's feet—especially the tiny, delicate-looking ones. First I give her a foot rinse, but then I suck on each toe individually. I get turned on by the femininity of them."

—Lisa Ann, 33

You don't have to be a detective to unravel the inner folds of the vagina. The best way to experiment is by checking yourself out first. Get out a small mirror, one that can stand on its own, and place it between your legs. Once you've got yourself wrapped around the mirror, position your body so that you have a great view of your beautiful vulva. Open your lips. Spread them apart with one hand and use the fingers of the other hand to lightly caress your clitoris. Use your fingers to explore inside the vaginal canal in search of your G-spot. There are lots of fun things to discover about the female body, and the best way to learn is through hands-on research.

No two vulvas are created equal—well, at least in terms of appearance. On the outside, every woman looks different. Just as men have long and short penises, some women have long, dark inner lips that hang outside their outer ones. Other women have barely any inner lips at all. A woman can have a large clitoris, one that peeks out from under the hood, or she can have one that stays neatly tucked away until she's ready to play. When you first go down on a woman, you won't know exactly what you're in for. But that's part of the mystery of being with a woman. Once things unfold, only then shall they truly be revealed.

Like being with a man, for some women being with another woman will teach them that size can matter. No two vaginas (as in vaginal canals) are going to be the same length, width, or tightness. One finger inside a smaller vagina is going to feel as tight as three or four fingers (or maybe the whole fist) in a larger one. This is something that you'll learn about your partner when you eventually explore there. But no matter what she can take, you want to make sure you're ready for anything.

CONSCIOUS CLITORIS

While you're playing around down there, here's something to remember. The clitoris has about 8,000 nerve fibers, meaning it has just as many nerve endings as the entire length of the penis! That's why clitorises can be really sensitive and sometimes uncomfortable if touched head-on. The clitoris also has a clitoral shaft, which can be found by gently pressing on the clitoral hood (it's rubbery and cordlike). And the clitoris has legs, or crura, that look like the wishbone you'd find in a turkey. The crura spread on either side of the vagina, just like the inner lips.

PERINEUM

The perineum is the region between the genitals and the anus. Like the anus, the perineum is one of those equal-opportunity areas, meaning that rubbing it not only feels good for a woman, but men like it, too!

THE COOLEST THING ABOUT THE CLITORIS IS THAT IT'S THE ONLY ORGAN IN THE HUMAN BODY DESIGNED FOR THE SOLE PURPOSE OF PLEASURE.

" The first time I was with a woman, it was a little awkward in the beginning. I wasn't sure if she'd like to be touched the way I touched myself. I didn't know exactly what to do. But we kissed and laughed and fondled each other's bodies, and then I did what felt natural."

—Lisa, 23

HOT SPOTS

When pleasuring a woman, it's important to hit the right spots. While playing with the clit may do the trick every time, three additional spots—the G-spot, the AFE (Anterior Fornix Erogenous) Zone, and the U-spot—may also come in handy when pleasing a woman.

G-SPOT

Named after the German gynecologist Ernst Gräfenberg, the G-spot is a dense collection of nerve endings located at the base of the urethral sponge behind the pubic bone, which is also known as the Skene's gland. The G-spot has been called the female prostate, and upon arousal, it engorges. Many doctors have argued that the G-spot does not exist, but the truth is, in order to find it, a woman must be highly aroused. It is approximately one to two finger beds in length (a finger bed is measured by the bends of each finger; each bend is one finger bed) inside the vagina and is best found by stroking toward the belly button, using one finger or two, in a come-hither sort of motion. It's about the size of a dime and has the texture of a walnut shell.

Of course, there are lots of other places to explore and many more details to discover. You can check out a woman's AFE Zone, located on the floor of her vagina (on the wall opposite the G-spot), or her U-spot, just outside and around her urethra. Other places will reveal themselves to you when the time is right.

" *The best thing about being with a woman is that it always feels familiar. It's like I'm finally with somebody who gets me. She knows what turns me on and what doesn't. She can read my body in a way that a man can't. She can also get me off in under ten minutes . . . well, most of the time.*"

—Erin, 25

FOR THE VERY FIRST TIME

The first time you sleep with another woman, you're fulfilling a fantasy. The fact that you're finally in this position, and not just dreaming about what could happen, means that you've probably given some thought to the things that turn you on. It's time to think about what it is you'd like another woman to do with, to, and for you. This is a good starting point for your first time, because while first times are exciting and invigorating, they can also be nerve-racking and scary. The first time you do anything, you're not sure what to expect. You don't have the confidence that builds up over time and with experience. You haven't done this before, so you're not quite sure what you're doing. But in order to get over that hump, and in order to enjoy the second and third times, you need to overcome that first hurdle.

If you're ready for the experience, you need to let yourself go there. Be ready to enjoy the fact that you're willing to try something new, or that you like something a little bit less vanilla, and go with that feeling. Be proud of yourself for not giving in to what others might expect from you. If you feel a sense of guilt because of your family's values, your upbringing, or whatever, acknowledge it, accept it, and then let it go.

Breathe.

Breathe again.

Breathe one more time.

Breathing is going to help you control your anxiety and get yourself into the groove so that you can go with the flow. And it's all about flow. Because whatever floats your boat deserves to float.

Being with a woman might afford you some of the most sensual and sexual experiences you've ever had. A lot of women are softer than their male counterparts. Many women have insider knowledge about what to do with a woman's body. Women know how they like to be touched, and can at least use that as a starting point for touching other women. They know the sweet spots that a man might miss. Their hands are softer, smoother, and more delicate. There's no itchy stubble to irritate your upper lip or brush against your inner ones.

" I find that most women I've been with consider their lips to be a highly erogenous zone. So when I first kiss a woman, I start gently, making sure our lips are just brushing up against one another..."

—Gina, 28

There are certain things that you should think about when you're having a first experience. The most important thing is to relax and remember that this isn't meant to be work, this is meant to be play. Make sure you know your own body before trying to figure out another woman's anatomy. Know if, and how, you like to rub your G-spot, or the types of strokes you like on or around your clitoris. Masturbation is probably the best way to figure out what you like and what you don't like.

Try to avoid alcohol or drugs the first time you're planning on getting it on with a woman. It's not that added stimulants can't make for a fun trip, but it's important to make sure you're doing what you're doing because you want to be there. You need to be present, not only for yourself but for your partner. Make eye contact. Find a touch that connects. There are lots of little things you can do to remain in the moment, whether it's the first, second, or fiftieth time you're with a woman.

"I usually start playing with myself in front of any new partner—man or woman. This way they can see what it is I like, and the types of moves that make me moan and groan. And then I ask them to do the same for me. I want our first time together to be enjoyable. I like a little guesswork, but I also like a little help."

—Jamie, 33

"I love when she looks at me as I touch her. It lets me know that she's there, with me, having the same experience. I mean, it's not the exact same experience for any two people, but at least we're connecting. If we can't connect, then the sex won't ever be that great. And I like great sex. Who doesn't, really?"

—Karen, 27

In addition, a lot of women do like sex toys, but sex toys shouldn't be the first things that come out of the drawer when you're with a woman. Spend your time, that first time, using your natural given talent (your mouth and your hands) to show your partner just how much you adore her. If you're not sure what to do, or even if you think you know, it's very important to communicate. Ask her how she likes to be touched or, if you can, have her show you. Ask her if she wants more or less of something and if things feel good or not so good. A big part of sex is communication.

It's also important to be realistic about your first experience. While it would be great if everything just clicked, odds are there will be some unexpected twists and turns. As with any first-time experience, it's all about discovery, and discovery is a learning process. What's important is that you're learning about what turns her on, what turns her off, and what works for the two of you. You're sharing an experience that will teach you things, things that you can use both alone and together. And that's valuable information.

So breathe.

Relax. Talk. Laugh. Get silly.

Get sloppy. Get into it.

4

ANATOMICALLY SPEAKING

The thing that's most interesting about being a woman is that our genital erogenous zones happen to be inside, or under, flaps, folds, and creases. While men get to see their genitals flopping around every single day of their lives, a woman's most delicate places are tucked neatly away, where they remain a mystery until we get to know who we really are. This makes our sexuality, and our ideas of sex, something we often guard; and when we are ready to give ourselves over to the experience, it is as much an inward experience as an outward one. Of course, erogenous zones aren't limited to our genitals, but the fact that our genitals are placed where they are does help us understand a bit more about how our sex lives eventually unfold. It can also explain why, as we develop into our sexual selves, we tend to be more open to certain experiences. Finding our true sexual nature can take quite a long while, but that's part of growing up.

TRIGGER ZONES

It's not only our genitals that turn us on. We have other trigger zones as well, such as the one that covers our entire body from head to toe (that would be our skin). Our breasts can also be highly sensitive, and a slight rub of the nipples has the potential to send us into orbit. For some of us, a playful bite on the arm might do little to turn us on, but suck on our inner thigh and we won't ask you to stop. It truly is different strokes for different folks. And while we can all agree that we have different "turn on" knobs and "turn off" ones, we can also all agree that no matter what, there's going to be some stroke, probe, or lick that does something to make us hot and bothered. Of course, before we can expect to get another woman off, we need to make sure we know how to find those hot buttons on our own bodies. That means we need to take time to get to know what's going on between our own thighs. We need to masturbate, and find out what feels good.

" Love was always the goal, and my point every step of the way was that nothing is wrong with love, no matter what flavor it comes in."

—Ani DiFranco,
singer/songwriter

MASTURBATION

Masturbation is not wrong, sinful, or dirty. It doesn't matter what you grew up believing or what you still believe. It's not something that will make you go blind or result in the death of cute kittens everywhere. Masturbation is a beautiful way to connect with your own body, to feel your unique physical structure, to understand the way you function. It's about providing your own pleasure and knowing that nobody else need be responsible for that. Masturbation is a healthy part of a relationship with your body. No matter whom you're with, it is not something that should be taken away from you, at any point or for any reason. And you shouldn't expect your partner to stop doing it, either. In fact, mutual masturbation is even hotter, because you get to touch yourself while you watch your partner play around as well. This shared masturbation will provide you details about how to love her body. Masturbation is a ritual, a form of worship, and it is you revering yourself.

" I think that the most important thing to know about getting a woman off is that you should focus on her entire body and stimulate everything. I think that a fully aroused woman is one of the hottest sexual encounters you can have. It is so satisfying to stimulate all the different parts of the female body. I love to hear a woman squeal as she becomes more and more aroused."

—Caryn, 26

Perhaps it's just a matter of touch-and-go, but if you're looking for ways to learn a bit more about your partner, you can start by initiating a mutual-masturbation session. Start by masturbating yourself, and tell her that you'd love to see what she likes to do, too. Ask for permission to watch her masturbate.

Or touch her body and ask her to place her hand on top of yours, and then she can gently guide you to the places she likes to be touched. It's better than being left to guess, especially if you're less confident about your own manual skills. Of course, with practice, improvement is virtually guaranteed. But for some of us, just getting over that first hump makes everything else more enjoyable, and a whole lot less stressful.

Or maybe you love to masturbate, and you're totally into the idea of watching each other get off. Maybe you've done your fair share of finger-licking research, but your other sexual experiences have been limited to playing with men. Well, let's just level the playing field here, shall we?

MASTURBATION MANEUVERS

Before you think about how to get her off, think about how you like to masturbate. What maneuvers do you use to take yourself to the point of no return? Is it a certain stroke, twist, or tap? What don't you like as well? It's not always easy to talk about sex, especially if you aren't sure how the person will respond. Telling someone what she's doing right or wrong can be draining, especially since our brains are such an important part of our sex life. Make sure you keep the conversation positive, no matter what you choose to say or what she says. Don't use words that criticize, even if you don't like what's going on. Instead, find a way to say, "Yes, but . . ." or "Can you do this instead?" Or ask a simple yet effective question, such as, "Does this feel good?" A simple yes or no would suffice, and it makes conversation quick, easy, and painless. And it will only help make the sex better, too!

" I love the way women feel and I love playing with breasts. There are probably many reasons for loving a woman's breasts. For starters, men don't have them. They're soft. They are unique and come in so many different shapes and sizes, and the nipples get hard when you lick them. I like to suck and gently bite and lick her nipples. I like to run my hands over them and squeeze them. I really like it when a woman is on top of me and leans her breasts into my mouth and sort of hits me with them."

—Stella, 32

"I would hope to get sexually nurtured from my experience with a woman and hope that she can experience this, too, and whatever else she might be looking for in her experience with me. I want to feel her soft skin and see her face as I give her pleasure. I love to use my hands on women. Women are beautiful."

—Jenn, 27

Women are beautiful. You are beautiful. This whole experience has the potential to be beautiful. Remember that, and when you're ready to go … here's a helping hand.

GIVING GOOD HAND

Masters and Johnson, two of the leading sex researchers of the twentieth century, spent a great deal of time studying female sexual response. Upon observing women masturbate, they noticed that women tended to focus their hands on the clitoral head, the shaft, their mound, and their inner and outer lips. Most women didn't directly stimulate the head of the clitoris until they were on the verge of orgasm, and prior to that, they were usually a little to the left or to the right.

Remember, it's always going to be a little different for every individual. Finding the right technique and rhythm is going to take a bit of patience and a bit more practice. Don't lose sight of the fact that you're here to have fun. It shouldn't feel like work, though perhaps maybe it's a little like research, and it shouldn't stress you out. Your goal is pleasure, and that's the same goal your partner has. And pleasure is all about fun.

Before you get started with your hands, think about what angle you'll take. While lying horizontally is the most common position to stimulate a woman, it doesn't have to be your only option. It's nice to have some pressure on the mons pubis (the mound) while playing with her genitals. You can rest the heel of your hand, which can include the wrist, right where her pubic hair meets the skin. It's good to relax your hand while you continue fiddling around. The first time you use your hands to get a woman off, you might experience fatigue and soreness in your fingers or wrist. With a guy you're using more of an up-and-down full-hand motion, but with a girl it's different. You're going to be more focused on one or two fingers, and you're going to rely heavily on some form of wrist action. It's okay to switch hands or alternate between your hands and another object, but the first time you get her off, it's nice to play with her with your hands for a while. This way you'll really get to know the landscape.

" A man did this to me once and I loved it so much that I like to try it on women now. Finger her with one or two fingers while the other hand presses gently on her lower abdomen. This brings the G-spot closer to the fingers already inserted inside her and it's the bomb!"

—Cristie, 34

" I like the way it feels to make a woman orgasm. It's more powerful than bringing a man to orgasm and it's definitely more involved. I like seeing and hearing a woman come in front of me—it's so much hotter than a man coming."

—Stacey, 32

THE TRACE

All women have a unique look and texture, and by familiarizing yourself with her majesty, you'll get to know the ins and outs of her palace. Tracing her box with your fingers is an easy way to get acquainted. Trace the outer lips, then open her up and trace the inner lips, the opening of her vagina, and the clitoris. You can also trace the trail from her fourchette to her anus, and circle your fingers lightly around her bum. Imagine that her vulva is a map full of buried treasure and that in order for you to find the gold, you've got to gently search for it.

UP AND DOWN, SIDE TO SIDE

Some women like it simple. A side-to-side motion over the clitoral hood is a nice way to start things out, since going side to side, as opposed to up and down, doesn't leave the clitoris feeling overly stimulated and vulnerable. Up-and-down motions might reveal too much of the clitoral hood before she's ready to make her debut, but either way, you can't go wrong with these simple and easy strokes. Using the pad of your index finger, or your index and middle fingers for more coverage, gently stroke the head of the clitoris.

CLITORAL CIRCLING

This is just one of many clitoral maneuvers, but it's quite simple. Using the pad of your index finger, gently move in circles around the clitoris, making sure to circle over the shaft. Start clockwise and then change it to counterclockwise. You can make slow, deliberate movements or rapid ones. You can even expand outward to include the vaginal lips as well, gently teasing her by not making it into the entrance of her vagina, only teasing her on the periphery.

EIGHT IS ENOUGH

Eight is enough is all about covering a larger area of the vulva, and by doing a figure eight, you can tease lots of her juicy bits. Start on the hood of the clit, at the shaft, and gently outline the number eight from the tip of the clitoris to the fourchette, and then up again, until you're back to where you started. Like the long version of clitoral circling, eight is all about coverage; but unlike the clitoral circles, it's all about going in two directions.

HEAD ROLLS AND TAPS

Gently roll the head of the clitoris between your thumb and index finger. You can roll with determination or relax and roll. You can also unroll and gently tap on the head of the clitoris. I find that I like tapping as I near orgasm, but different strokes work differently for every individual.

ALL HANDS ON DECK

Spread the lips apart with the aid of the thumb and index finger. Use the index finger of the other hand to play with the clitoris. You can also do this with one hand, by spreading the lips with the thumb and middle finger and using the index finger for stimulation.

TIP: THE THUMB IS THE STRONGEST AND FATTEST OF THE FIVE FINGERS, SO DOING ANY OF THESE TECHNIQUES WITH YOUR THUMB WILL ADD PRESSURE AND COVER MORE SURFACE AREA.

FOUR FINGERS AND A THUMB

Your thumb should be placed inside her vulva, playing with her G-spot. The four other fingers should be lightly covering her clitoris, moving in a back-and-forth motion (think windshield wiper) over her clitoris. This provides dual stimulation for the receiver.

PENETRATE-HER

What's nice about going inside her vagina while you do any of the above on her clitoris is that "finger-fucking" provides extra stimulation. We'll discuss more techniques that combine hand and mouth in the next chapter, "Speaking in Tongues," but for now, know that it's nice to put a finger inside her. The first third of the vagina is the most sensitive, so shallow, gentle touches are sometimes more seductive than deep, hard thrusts.

HANDY HELPERS

• MAKE SURE YOUR NAILS ARE WELL TRIMMED AND CLEAN. NOBODY WANTS DIRTY FINGERNAILS NEAR THEIR MOST PRECIOUS OF PLACES.

• LUBE IS NOT ALWAYS NECESSARY, BUT IT CAN PLAY AN IMPORTANT ROLE IN MANUAL STIMULATION. STICK WITH A WATER-BASED LUBE, PREFERABLY WITHOUT GLYCERIN (A SUGAR AND POSSIBLE IRRITANT), TO MAKE SURE THINGS GO SMOOTHLY.

• LATEX GLOVES ARE A HOT OPTION FOR SAFER HAND SEX.

• MAKE EYE CONTACT. LET HER KNOW THAT YOU'RE THERE, WITH HER, IN THE MOMENT.

• FOLLOW HER LEAD. BODY LANGUAGE WILL TELL YOU A LOT ABOUT WHAT SHE LIKES AND WHAT SHE DOESN'T LIKE.

TALK DIRTY TO ME

A lot of women lack self-confidence when it comes to their bodies and both giving and receiving pleasure. Many of us grow up believing that our vaginas aren't clean, and that we aren't perfect because one breast is larger than the other or our inner lips hang below our outer ones. Because we don't like something about ourselves, we sometimes lack confidence and self-esteem. Being deficient in self-assurance leads us to not always feeling beautiful, or special, or important, which can cause us to ignore the sexual satisfaction that we want or deserve. So, in order to encourage a warm, trusting sexual relationship, it's nice to add the element of dirty talk to our experiences. While it's not always easy to say how you feel, a few simple words or moans can do wonders for your sex life and for her sexual self-esteem. If you or your lover isn't comfortable with words such as "pussy" or "box," don't use them. Instead, focus on subtle phrases such as "down there" and "between your thighs." Sure, they sound less specific than those other terms, but it's still going to sound hot and sexy if you really mean it.

If dirty talk doesn't do it for you, or even if it does, there are other things to do to set the mood. Lighting can work wonders to make a woman feel sexier, especially low-wattage bulbs or a bulb with a red or purple tinge. (Reds and purples do a lot to add that "parlorlike/bordello" feel, and they can really help set a mood.) Also, if you're going to make it in the bedroom, sheets with a high thread count always enhance the moment. Plus, a variety of pillows will help with positions, and flowers and candles help set a romantic mood. No matter what you add or subtract from your experience, this is about relaxation and enjoyment. It's about mutual pleasure and discovery. And it's also about living in the moment—so live!

DIRTY GIRL: EXAMPLES OF SOME PHRASES YOU CAN USE

- I can't wait to spread your legs and go down there.

- You have such a beautiful body, I can't wait to taste you.

- The thought of getting you off turns me on.

- You have the smoothest, softest skin, and I just want to rub up against you.

- I've been thinking about spreading your legs for a very long time.

- You're so sexy, and I'm so lucky.

- I want to run my fingers over your clitoris and feel your lips quiver.

- You have such a pretty pussy.

- I can't wait to put my face between your thighs and watch you moan.

- I've dreamed about putting my hand inside your box all night.

5

SPEAKING IN
TONGUES

OPEN UP AND SAY "AAAAH"

You've dipped your fingers into the lovely, luscious world of woman, and it was as warm, sweet, and comforting as you knew it would be. You relished the uniqueness of the landscape of her canal, the bits and bumps of her clitoris, and the soft, silky smoothness of her body. You enjoyed the hands-on experience of being with a woman, and now you've decided to take it one step further. It's finally time to taste her.

There are certain things you're going to want to think about before you put your head between her legs. You want to remember that this is all about comfort, connection, and communication. That being said, it's best to make sure you maintain a comfortable position for oral sex, especially since going down may mean that you'll be gone for a while.

It's also a good idea to use pillows to prop her vagina up toward your face. In addition, you might want to sample the goods and kiss her lips and her clitoris (no tongue) before you go all out, just so you know what to expect. It's okay to be nervous about going down on a woman the first time you do it. It's not something you've done before. Even if you're not nervous, it's still best to start out slowly and progressively work your tongue up into a writhing frenzy. Just like when using your fingers, you need to remember that women are aroused gradually and that if you go down on a woman when she's not entirely ready, or you press a little too hard, it's not going to feel as good as if you gently taunt and tease her.

" My favorite thing about giving head is knowing that my tongue is at the controls when it comes to directing her pleasure. It's like I'm a captain, and I'm steering the ship. I also love getting head from a woman. Her face is so baby soft that I don't have to worry about stubble, and it's nice to look down to see this beautiful feminine form being able to provide me with so much pleasure."

—Arianna, 25

THE TONGUE IS MIGHTIER THAN THE SWORD

There's no denying that oral sex relies heavily on the tongue, but it's not the only part of your body you'll use. Oral sex is about bringing your whole face (including your nose, your upper lip, your tongue, and your eyes), as well as your hands, along for the ride.

If adult movies actually showed you the proper way to go down on a woman, all you'd see is the back of the giver's neck. Oral sex is less about tongue and more about using your entire face on her box.

The tongue is also one of the most important elements in oral sex. With it you will determine how you want to go down on a partner. Will you use flat strokes or pointed ones? Will you use the top of the tongue or flip it up and use its less-known underside? Will you flick the clitoris with your tongue or draw gentle circles on her nub? There are lots of things to do with your tongue, but the first step is recognizing how to use it.

So how will you use your tongue? You don't want to start out directly on the head; instead, you should start by focusing more attention on the whole vulva. Do small licks from the bottom of her vagina up to the top, or from top to middle, or middle to bottom. Or vary those types of long, slow, flat licks. Focus on the bits and pieces of her body that are easy to grab onto with your lips—don't use teeth here—such as the inner lips, or maybe even the outer ones. Eventually move up to the clitoris, but don't spend too much time directly on it, at least not yet; you need to build up to that one. You can also use your tongue to explore her vagina, stick it in and out, so that she experiences the soft sensations only your tongue can provide. You can press on her mound to gently reveal her clitoris as she gets more aroused. Use the underside of your tongue if you get tired—for some women this is an easier way to give head for a longer amount of time. As she gets really aroused, try flicking on the clitoris, and see if she likes it. Eventually, you'll want to add a hand, either in her vagina or around the opening of it. You can even leave a finger on the fourchette for extra pressure. Whatever you decide, you can experiment the first, second, third, and thirtieth time you're with a woman.

TIP: The pubococcygeus muscle, or PC muscle, stretches from the pubic bone to the tailbone. A well-developed and exercised PC muscle can help enhance sex and orgasm, help prevent urinary incontinence, and make childbirthing (and recovery) easier. "Kegel" is the name of the exercises you do to strengthen your PC muscle. You can find the muscle by stopping the flow of urine the next time you go to the bathroom. But once you find it, you don't want to keep doing that. Instead, practice using that muscle at other times of the day. Start by doing three sets of ten reps daily, then keep increasing your workout. You can also buy a Kegel exerciser to help you with your routine. Try Natural Contours Energie or Betty Dodson's Barbell on for size.

THE MAKINGS OF AN ORAL MASTERPIECE

Oral sex happens in three stages. The first stage is **The Tease**, where you gently and gingerly begin to play with your partner's vulva. Of course, you don't want to hit her hot spot just yet. In the beginning you want to kiss her inner thighs, her toes, her belly, and other places; but when you eventually make it down to her temple, you want to start out with a loving, delicate kiss. This is a good time for you to get used to your surroundings. Smell her vulva. What does it smell like? Kiss it with your lips. What does it taste like? Give it even more kisses—long, slow, wet ones, sort of as you might have done when you first learned to kiss your pillow. This will give you a general idea of the smell, taste, and feel of your lover's vagina, and it's a good jumping-off point from which you can further explore. After you've taunted and tempted her, it's time to bring out the tongue. Start softly and gently; you don't want to apply too much pressure until you know she's ready. Really get into it, get into her essence, her arousal process. Remember that you're not just doing this for her, you're doing this for you as well. You want this experience, and you want to get the most out of the pleasure, when it comes to both giving and receiving. In the end, it's about an ecstatic moment that the two of you will share.

"I love the taste of a woman and the juices that come from her. But all women have such a unique taste, so I can't say exactly what they taste like! One of my favorite things is to use my 'under' tongue to rub on an exposed clitoris; it seems to have a very stimulating effect."

—Kelli, 35

The best time to find out what your partner likes and what she doesn't like is during the tease. This is the time to try any number of strokes, including any of the ones you can do with your hand. But instead of your hand, you're now substituting your tongue. You may be asking yourself how you will know whether or not she likes something, but body language can tell you a lot about a person. Think about the things you do when you're enjoying cunnilingus. Odds are they are similar to what she'll do. She might lift her pelvis and grind it into your face, while her back stays flat on the bed. She might moan and make thrusting actions. She might just lie still and rub your head. If she doesn't like it, she'll probably back away from your tongue or make no attempt at touching you or connecting.

The tease will help you find your groove, which is the second stage to good oral sex. Establishing **The Groove** will lead you to your rhythm. If you sit back and reflect on what gets you off, it's often all about the motion and the pacing. When someone is going down on you and you like what she's doing, you want her to keep doing that same thing. Sure, you might want it faster, harder, or softer, or maybe a little to the left or to the right, but no matter what you want, once she has the motion, you don't want her to change it. The tease is a good place to play with the change, but the groove is a good time to keep going in perpetual motion. During the groove, you're more "clitcentric," and you might experiment with a few different techniques, but you don't want to completely stop and start the action—unless, of course, your goal is to never get past the tease. Once you get your groove on, it's good to keep on movin'—don't stop!

"The most important thing for me is to ask the woman what she likes. Different women definitely do have certain things that work particularly well for them. My best sex, regardless of the gender, is with people who know what they like and ask for it."

—Stacey, 32

This will lead you to **The Finale**, also known as the grand climax or orgasm. You've established the techniques that work best for her. You're in a comfortable position and so is she. She's tugging at your hair and closing your face off with her thighs. She's obviously riding high, and you want to take her even higher. It's time to make her come. The trick here is in how you're going to do it. It's a good time to incorporate some hand action into your play. Of course, if at any point in the groove you get tired, as long as you keep it wet, you can substitute a hand for a tongue. But with the tease (buildup) and the groove (establishment), you will undoubtedly find techniques that will help you last a little longer. This time, instead of using your hand on her clitoris, you might want to consider sticking a finger or two inside her vagina, in order to play with her G-spot. Now's a good time to go searching for her G-spot, because odds are that after all the foreplay you've had, she's good and ready, and highly aroused.

As you massage the G-spot, you want to also focus on the clitoris. At this point it's okay to stick with one or two basic techniques that seem to really make her writhe. You should continue doing this until she can't take it any longer, and then she might just explode in your mouth.

FINDING THE G-SPOT

1. For starters, make sure she's really ready, meaning she's excited and revving to go (translation: highly aroused). You won't be able to find the G-spot otherwise.

2. The easiest position for her to be in is on her back, with her legs spread, knees bent.

3. Slip a finger (or two) up into her vagina. Even though the G-spot is the urethral sponge, you still have to masturbate it through the anterior wall of the vagina.

4. When you stick a finger into her vagina, it should be approximately one to two finger beds (in length). Move your finger in a come-hither sort of motion. Think "up and around," or that you're bringing your finger back toward the clitoris or the belly button.

5. When you hit the spot, it will be about the size of a dime or quarter and have the texture of a walnut shell. You can use back-and-forth motions on it or around it, or even try circles. You'll need to apply a little pressure in order for her to feel what's going on inside her.

6. She may feel that she has to urinate. That's okay. Either let her go pee or have her just relax through it. Keep licking her clitoris while you play with her G-spot.

7. Keep rubbing the G-spot until she comes. She may squeeze her PC muscle while you masturbate her clitoris. You'll feel a sucking sensation if she does it. Using your PC muscle during penetration can heighten an orgasm.

ASSUMING THE POSITION

There are plenty of ways to go about having oral sex, and in any standard position there are going to be a number of variations to try. The positions below are but a few suggestions of how to do it. You'll have to play around to figure out what works best for you and what doesn't, but the only way to know what works is to try, try, and try.

READ BETWEEN THE THIGHS
Possibly the simplest and most relaxed position for the receiver to be in is lying comfortably on her back. She might be propped up with a soft pillow under her head and another one under her buttocks. By raising her pelvis with a pillow, you'll have VIP access to her vulva. The woman receiving cunnilingus has a few options when it comes to spreading her legs. She can leave them flat, and you can lie between them, or she can bend them at the knees, or even place them on your shoulders, as long as it's comfortable for you. Of course, you can also press her legs back, toward her chest, and go to town that way. If you want to draw her legs closer to your body, you should wrap your arms around her thighs.

The giver can also lie perpendicular to the receiver in this position. This allows you to use her legs as your own pillow, and will provide you with a new view of her vulva. This is a good position to access all of her vulva, from her fourchette up to her mound.

ABOUT FACE
Basically, the person receiving oral sex squats or kneels over your face, placing her knees on both sides of your head. In this position, she is straddling you. She can either face you or turn away, depending on the angle both you and she prefer. If you happen to be near a headboard or any other object that is easy to lean on, the one getting head should lean her chest and/or arms on it. This will help you out in the end, because it will allow you to adjust the pressure on your face, leaving you feeling a little less confined. The woman on top should grind her hips, lift and lower her vagina, and tilt her pelvis. She is essentially the dominant one in this position, so it's not going to work for you if you don't want to lose control of the situation or if it's your first time and you want to be the one to call the shots.

DOGGY DOES IT
Doggy style generally feels good during intercourse, so why not give it a go during oral sex? While the receiver is on all fours, you can lick her from behind. It may not be the easiest position to stay in, but it's a good way to get lots of access to both her vulva and her buttocks. In addition, this position is playful. The receiver can also lean forward on her front arms while raising her ass high in the air. In another form of the same position, the giver can lie under her, sort of like the "About Face," only she's not actually sitting on your face or applying any pressure. This gives you a chance to play with her dangling breasts and her vagina all at once.

SIT DOWN AND SPREAD 'EM

This position is done sitting down, maybe on the edge of the bed or on a chair, or you can even try the couch, if it's a comfortable one. You kneel, squat, or crouch in front of your partner (if it's a low chair, you might even be able to sit) and practice your skills from this perspective. The person receiving head can place her feet on the floor, spread her legs ever so slightly, or spread them wide. She can also place her legs over your shoulders or wrap them around your lower back.

STANDING POSE

This is a great one if you want to live out some hot fantasy or role-play. If she's standing and you're kneeling or sitting in front of her, there's definitely a power dynamic going on. I like to think of this pose as a great one in which to worship your partner. She stands against a wall, counter, or some sort of concrete structure or object, and you go down before her. Maybe she even holds your head and guides you toward her genital area. In this position, I really like starting out by kissing her toes, worshipping her feet, and then working my way up her legs until I eventually make it to her temple. Take your time. Appreciate the goddess in all her beauty.

"My favorite position is to have her standing and braced up against a wall. This way I can see almost her entire body, and it's a great position to make and maintain eye contact. Plus, for me, it's the best position to find the right spots to lick."

—Trina, 34

TWO TO TANGO

There are pros and cons to mutual pleasure. The biggest pro is that you're both receiving generous amounts of loving and touching at the same time. The biggest con is that it can be really distracting, and if you focus on getting pleasure, it's not always as easy to give. It can also be difficult for the woman on top to support herself for a long period of time. And it can be awkward for both of you if there's a big difference in size. But for some it's just about fun, and doubling your pleasure is, indeed, all about enjoyment.

While it can be a distraction for some, others find this one to be a favorite. In **Traditional 69**, one partner lies on top of the other (but in a reverse position), so that each woman can easily play with the genitals of the other. For the woman on the bottom, prop a pillow or two under your head, and possibly your hips, to allow for a more comfortable and accessible position.

In this position, it's also possible to alternate pleasure without having to change locations. Even if one person needs a break, the other can continue to build up the momentum.

On Your Side is by far a more relaxed position for 69. The two of you lie side by side, both between the other person's legs. Using her lower leg as a pillow to support your head, you fondle and frolic in her genitals. Wrap your arms around her top leg and suck away!

AFTERGLOW

No matter how you decide to come, or even whether or not you do, it's important to remember to spend some quality time just relaxing in each other's arms. So much of sex happens after sex, and we need to bear in mind that a person needs to feel validated, nurtured, and cared for after sharing an intimate part of herself with you. Unless you are in a relationship where this doesn't work, and it's been talked about and agreed upon, it's nice to spend at least a few minutes providing your partner with attention. A little love can go a long way.

If you're alone, a toy can usually help you achieve orgasm more easily and quick. Perhaps you've never had an orgasm, or it takes you a long time to come; a toy can help you figure out what you like. Maybe you'd like to explore certain areas that you just can't reach with a finger or a tongue. Or maybe you're just curious about what it feels like to use something that vibrates, or rotates, or curves to hit your G-spot.

Most women who decide to test out toys, at some point or another, buy a vibrator or a dildo. Vibrators are fun to use alone or on another woman, especially on or around the clitoris, because they can provide a nice, steady, or intense sensation. Dildos are nice to use inside a woman, since they can provide her with some deeper, more penetrative loving that she may not be able to get from other parts of another woman's body (unless you use a fist). Plus, strapping a dildo into a harness can add a new level of sexual excitement and intimacy to your relationship.

THE VIBRATIONAL PULL

Vibrators are commonly referred to as body massagers or back massagers. They help women achieve orgasms more quickly, more often, and with more strength and intensity than hands or mouths alone ever can.

Doctors invented the first electrically powered vibrators back in the late 1800s in order to help treat women with hysteria, a disease that's as outdated as getting a vibrational rubdown from an M.D. The treatment for those women included masturbating them to orgasm, which is exactly what doctors did with their first vibrating machines. Soon home models appeared, and there were even advertisements for some of these rather large and heavy machines in places such as the Sears, Roebuck Catalogue *and* Needlecraft *magazines. The ads disappeared as more and more vibrators made their debut in adult cinema, and they were no longer publicly touted after the 1920s.*

Today there are a myriad of vibrators on the market. Some buzz, some pulse, some do tricks such as light up or rotate in circles. Some have variable speeds and some don't. Some are just for clitoral stimulation and others have a slight curve in order to be inserted into the vagina to titillate the G-spot. Some have two heads and others have three. You can use a different vibrator every day for a month and find something slightly different in each model.

There are a couple of things you want to consider when purchasing a vibrator. Do you want one that functions with only one speed, or do you want the option of multiple levels of excitement? Should your vibrator be made of a hard plastic material (these tend to have the most powerful vibrations), or do you prefer a softer, more jellylike feel? Do you want a vibrator that can be inserted inside you, or is it something you'll use only for clitoral stimulation? Or perhaps you want something for both. What kind of batteries will it take, or will it plug in? How will it sound?

The most hyped vibrator in the sex-toy community is the Hitachi Magic Wand. Dubbed the "Cadillac of vibrators," the Magic Wand is a powerful plug-in back massager that works well for powerful clitoral stimulation. Because of its really intense vibration, a lot of women use the Magic Wand over their panties, or even over a blanket or a sheet. It's also good to use with a partner, because you can both press your clits against the head of the vibe and get off together.

Other popular vibrators include the Pocket Rocket and its waterproof sister, the Water Dancer, a small, simple one-speed vibrator that brings on a powerful punch. Made of hard plastic, it's not the vibe for everyone, but it has a loyal following. Then there are dual-action vibes such as the Rabbit Habit and the Magic Spot, both providing rotation, penetration, and clitoral stimulation at the same time. Of course, the best thing to do is experiment with a vibe and figure out if it works for you. It's all about what kind of action you want and what kind of stimulation you want to provide for your partner.

" My favorite toy is the strap-on. I have never received the pleasures of a harness, but I do love to give! The harness is very important. Make sure it holds the dildo firmly against your body so that you can give effective thrusts, and at an angle suitable to hit the right spots. I love vibrators, too. The Hitachi Magic Wand and the Rabbit are beyond words. If you have never been tied up and had someone force orgasm after orgasm on you with a toy, you haven't fully lived."

—Maria, 24

A dildo is a great companion in a women-loving-women relationship, because it can provide a deeper connection—at least deeper than you can often get by using hands alone. There's nothing hotter than strapping on a harness, wearing a beautiful bright-blue penis, and penetrating another woman with it. In fact, it not only looks hot, and can feel good for both parties involved, it also provides additional power play for the person doing the penetrating. Think about it. It's a combination of both feminine and masculine energy, and that in itself is a very powerful thing.

STRAP-ONS

Dildos can be used in conjunction with a harness, and when the two are put together, it's often referred to as "strap-on sex." The harness holds the dildo in place, which means that it keeps it pressed against the skin of the woman giving the pleasure. A harness can be worn around the hips, but there are also harnesses designed for thighs (because leg muscles are strong), chins, and wrists. Harnesses come with one strap or two, and it's up to the person wearing it to decide which is more comfortable. A one-strap generally fits more snugly, but it limits access to her genitalia during coreplay. Harnesses, like dildos and vibrators, come in a variety of styles and colors. You can find them in leather or nylon, rubber or plastic—it's all about preference.

THE BUZZ (SOME VIBRATORS YOU MAY WANT TO TRY):

HITACHI MAGIC WAND
POCKET ROCKET
VIBRATEX RABBIT HABIT
BLUEBERRY BUZZ
ULTIME
REMOTE BUTTERFLY
ORCHID G
LAYA
GIGOLO
IRIS
JE JOUE

SLIP-'N'-SLIDE

Lubrication is also a really important sex-toy accoutrement to have on hand at all times. While most women lubricate upon arousal, it's not guaranteed. In the 1994 *Sex in America* survey, 20 percent of women said they had trouble lubricating naturally. Now, the fact that she doesn't lubricate, or that you're using a hard dildo that needs some lubricant on it to slide right in, doesn't mean one or both parties aren't turned on. It just means that she might not naturally lube, or she could be on antidepressants, the birth-control pill, or something else is affecting her hormones. Therefore, it's best to always have lube around.

The best lubes are either water or silicone-based, but saliva is also a lube, even though it dries out rather quickly, which makes it less effective than store-bought brands. Whatever you decide, it should be a lube that will only add to your pleasure.

THE LOWDOWN ON LUBES

Some of the best lubes on the market are water or silicone based. Both are condom compatible (latex and polyurethane). Some of the best water-based lubes out there are Sensual Power and Astroglide. Certain water-based lubes contain glycerin—a sugar—so if you or she is prone to yeast infections, you may want to avoid buying a lube with glycerin. Sensual Power is glycerin-free, tasteless, and odorless. Silicone-based lubes tend to be more expensive, but they'll last a lot longer. The downer is that silicone lubes won't wash off without soap and water. Pink, one of the newer silicone lubes on the market, comes in an elegant bottle and contains vitamin E and aloe vera, both good, natural moisturizers. Another popular silicone lube is Eros, and there are a number of varieties on the market.

TIP: Use a condom if you're going to use a silicone-based lube with your silicone toy. The lube will cause a chemical reaction with these materials, causing the toy to change shape or disintegrate.

SHOP GIRL

Toys come in any number of shapes, styles, sizes, and colors, and it's not as if you can just pick out one toy and know it's going to be perfect. You'll probably want to peruse a list of female-friendly stores and figure out what works best for you. If you're planning on sharing your toys, I highly recommend silicone ones—safe and easy to clean—and they generally come in the largest variety of colors (some even have glitter). Regardless of which toy you decide on, sharing toys means that you should make sure to practice safer sex. That means putting a condom over your toy before you let somebody else play with it. That way, even if it's silicone, you can make sure that you aren't sharing anything else.

What you want to look for when purchasing a toy has to do with personal taste and preference. If you're shopping for a vibrator or a dildo for yourself, you want to look at the size of the toy—meaning the length, width, and girth—and find a size that you know will satisfy you. Make sure the toy you buy is a toy you feel. If it's a vibrator, you really want to figure out what the vibration might be like. You can test it out on your nose or your wrist if you happen to be in a store that has samples on display. Otherwise, you should ask the advice of friends or sex educators. The harder the material, the more it will vibrate. A plug-in vibe will also be more powerful than a battery-operated device. If you're shopping for a dildo and harness, you may want to find a store that allows you to try one on over your clothing. That way you can find one that fits comfortably and will allow you the freedom to move around during sex.

7

THREE'S
COMPANY

THREE IS NOT A CROWD

Life is full of self-discovery, and you've discovered that you like women, you like to be with other women, and now you think that you might want to share the experience of being with a man and another woman at the same time. You think if a twosome's sweet (like hot fudge and ice cream), a threesome might be even sweeter (like adding whipped cream and a cherry!). And, yeah, a threesome can be some of the most exciting sex you ever have. It can be magical and monumental, beautiful and breathtaking, naughty and nice. It can also be a disaster if things get out of control. So remember these key things to ensure a happy outcome: Nobody is a mind reader and communication is key. Threesomes can be a lot of fun, especially since there are more people in on the action; and the attention isn't always focused on one of two people. However, this same advantage can also be a disadvantage, because threesomes can be a lot more work than you might be prepared to handle. If you get easily jealous or you aren't ready to commit to being with your boyfriend or husband and another woman, you shouldn't do it. The experience is successful only if all the parties involved want to be there, and if you're able to talk with your partners about your expectations and your limits.

THE ARRANGEMENT

When you're ready to move ahead with the experience, you want to properly plan your threesome. Yeah, sex is about spontaneity and excitement, but in a situation where egos and hearts can be broken, it's best to take it step by step. If you're in a relationship, the first thing you want to do is talk with your partner about the idea of having a threesome. Gauge interest. If your partner doesn't seem all that turned on and into

it, don't do it. If he or she does, then continue the discussion by telling him or her why you want to bring another woman into your relationship. Explore your fantasies, use erotic language, and reassure your partner that no matter what happens, this experience is about the two of you—together.

If you're single, finding yourself in a threesome can be a whole lot easier. You don't have to explain to anybody why you want to do this, you only have to know it for yourself. What you need to think about is how you're going to be part of the experience and how you are going to make sure the experience is about fun, for everyone.

THE EVENT

As a single woman, you're going to have a much easier time engaging in sex with another couple. If you're part of a couple, you and your partner need to communicate your desires and make sure that you bring a third person in who can mutually provide for both of you.

Perhaps you'll meet at a party, a bar, online, or through friends. When you're ready to take your relationship to the next level, you want to ensure that this sexual experience is going to erotically rock your world. The best thing to do is know, from the beginning, what page everyone is on. If there's something with which you're not comfortable, don't wait for it to happen before you say something. If you know that one partner is feeling a little nervous, make sure to spend time focused on his or her relaxation at the start. You want to make sure that the space you're in isn't a negative head space (remember—the brain is the most powerful sex organ), because unenthusiastic thoughts can ruin this experience.

It's best to talk before you get into the bedroom (or whatever room you choose to do it in). Once you've talked and worked out any logistics that need to be worked out, start slowly. Don't rush—remember, this is an event, a fantasy turned reality, a bonus scene in your sex life. You want to take it slowly, appreciate the moments, and proceed with caution.

As things get heated, make sure you're playing fairly. You don't want to leave anyone out or have someone feel that he or she doesn't belong. You want to spend equal amounts of time on each person, and when you're sharing the responsibilities of giving, you want to share fairly.

It's important that all threesome participants be attracted to one another. Sure, one person might seem more pleasing to your palate, but you've come to play with two, and therefore it's two people you'll need to please. While you're probably more accustomed to having sex with your boyfriend, this is a special occasion where a woman is also part of your sexual feast, so savor the flavor and enjoy the experience of sharing what you've learned about pleasing a woman.

Again, take your time and don't rush to the finish line. The grand finale might be full-blown intercourse, or it might be oral sex, or even just an orgasm through masturbation, but don't be in a hurry to get there. Enjoy the kissing, the giggling, the caressing of new skin, and the excitement of first touch. Take pleasure in the tangled feet, the focused attention, the giving and receiving.

THREE-WAYS: TIPS AND TECHNIQUES TO SHOW YOU THE WAY

The following scenarios are examples of positions to try when three's the magic number.

ALL ABOUT ORAL

He's going down on his girlfriend while she's going down on their new friend. If you lie in a circle, using one another's legs as pillows, you can even make it one big oral circle, and the second girl can be giving him head while getting head from his girlfriend. Otherwise, one girl can sit on the face of the other girl, getting head from her while she lies on her back, wrapping her legs on his shoulders (or placing her legs on the bed for the most traditional style of oral sex), and receives oral sex from him. Ultimately, he's enjoying watching and participating in giving pleasure while the two of them relish in receiving. Either way, it's all about oral, and both women are experiencing the intense pleasure of some mouth-to-face action.

ONE LOVE

You focus all your attention on one person. Whoever that lucky person is will lie on his or her back, so that the head, neck, and breasts (or chest) can get as easily caressed as the genitals. While one person is going down on "the one," the other person can easily be sucking her toes or biting his nipples.

FROM BEHIND

She's on all fours, having intercourse doggy style with the man while licking the genitals of the other woman, who's facing the man as he engages the first woman. The woman receiving oral sex can then use her hands to hold on to the man and her mouth to kiss his lips as he continues to penetrate the other woman.

"Threesomes are about fantasy and reality . . . It's a beautiful thing when you're having fun and sharing something new. My girlfriend loves touching other women, and I love watching her doing what she loves. It's the most erotic thing I can think of."

—Scott, 29

REVERSE COWGIRLS

He's lying on his back, engaging one of the women in a reverse cowgirl position (she's on top with her behind and back toward his face). She can also be on top facing him if she wants to watch, and touch, more of the action. The other woman is sitting on his face, controlling just how his tongue hits her genitals. In the face forward position, the two women can extend their arms and caress each other, and they can also kiss.

BONDAGE À GO-GO

One of the women is blindfolded and tied to the bed, while the other woman and the man provide her with intense kisses and all sorts of pleasure. You can use a vibrator on the submissive woman or explore her nether regions with your fingers, lick her genitals and her nipples, or suck on her toes. If you're really adventurous, you can even doubly penetrate her, having the man engage her in one orifice while the woman could apply a strap-on and engage her in another. It's hot because one woman is giving into the pleasure of the two other participants.

When it's all over, you have one more decision to make. How long will you bask in the afterglow? How much time are you going to spend relaxing, surrounded by the pleasure that has been bestowed upon you? Are all three of you going to spend the night, or is the time after sex time for the couple to reconnect and reaffirm their love and commitment? These are all decisions you need to make together, but they are decisions the couple might want to talk about before involving a third party. Even if, as a couple, you feel comfortable having your play partner stay the night, it's still ultimately a decision that's best to make before you play.

POTENTIAL MÉNAGE À TROIS MISTAKES

If there is one golden rule to having a threesome, it is to play well with others. Sharing and playing fairly are the best ways to make sure everybody feels included. However ideal you want the outcome to be, it's not always easy to execute the perfect plan. Oftentimes something comes up at the last minute, and things have to be decided on the spot. And while a committed, communicative ménage à trois can work itself out, it's best to be aware that accidents do happen.

There are a lot of things that can happen that might not feel as right as you'd hoped they would. Your boyfriend might be going down on the other woman when he should be paying attention to you, or you might feel that the two of them are doing a little too much kissing and cuddling. Or maybe you're the other woman and you're not feeling all that included in the couple action; in fact, you're feeling as if they've forgotten you exist. Whatever it is that you're feeling, you aren't the only person who's ever experienced these emotions. The first thing is not to panic. It will only make the situation or relationship worse.

Next, it's best to think about what it is that's turning you off and figure out the best way to approach the situation. Before you blurt something out such as, "Stop, this is wrong," figure out what about "this" is wrong, and how you want to go about fixing things. If you can't think of a clear solution, you can start by saying that you aren't feeling all that comfortable at the moment, or that while you know this is fun, would it be okay if all three of you talked for a minute? Even if you're unhappy with the way your partner is devouring the latest addition to your sex life, you don't want to single him or her out right now. Remember, when our passion button is turned up, it's easy to take things much more seriously and feel more vulnerable. At this point, you will need to approach the situation with sensitivity. If you feel the need to stop the action, make sure to talk in a calm and caring manner. Perhaps all of you maintain some sort of touch as you talk. If you think there's no going back, or forward, you can always say that you're not feeling well and that while you're having fun, you think that you're going to need to take a rain check on the rest of the evening. While it will definitely be a downer, it's okay to keep your needs in check, too.

If you feel that the situation is manageable and that, while things aren't going exactly as planned, you're still having fun, it's okay to make a mental note of how you'd want things to be next time. After the evening has ended or, better yet, the next morning at breakfast, you and your partner can reassess what worked and what didn't work. If you are the single woman in the situation, you can go home and think about what you liked about the experience and what you didn't, and evaluate how you'd approach the situation next time.

It's important not to accuse anyone of anything. Don't blame one person for focusing too much or too little attention on one party or the other. Don't be upset if your partner makes that cute little scrunched-up orgasm face when another person is pleasuring him or her, because, odds are, if they're turned on, they're going to make that face. It's important to keep your jealousy in check and remember that engaging in this ménage à trois was your decision, too. Of course, if after having a threesome you realize that it's just not for you, that's also okay; but don't go blaming anybody for what didn't go your way.

In a threesome, there is no one way things can go.

8

THE MAGIC
GARDEN

A STATE OF MIND

You've thought about being with a woman. You've even started to do the research to set the plan in motion. You love the idea of being able to identify with your feminine self by finding ways to connect with other females. You think about having a same-sex experience, and you are pretty sure that you will find it empowering, but you're still not feeling completely confident in your decision.

You are not alone in how you feel. In fact, even after you have the experience, you may have some doubts about your reasoning or even your sexuality. That's totally normal, and it's more than okay. In fact, being with another woman will likely bring up some of your own issues and judgments. It might challenge what you perceive to be your definitive sexuality. It's important to remember that experimenting is experimenting. If you identify yourself as a heterosexual woman, loving another woman does not make you bisexual or a lesbian; it just makes you open. You can and will still identify yourself as a heterosexual woman, no matter what the experience, if that's indeed how you feel. What it can do is help you think about what you find sexy and what you have the potential to find attractive. It might challenge your values, or your family's values, and make you question everything you once believed in. But it's always better to regret something you did than something you never did, as long as it isn't physically hurting somebody in the process. And after this experience, you won't necessarily regret anything.

" Women are magic. A woman has the power to transform me from an ordinary girl into a goddess. She has the ability to make me feel weak or strong. A woman can get me to beg for mercy or beg for more. There's nothing, for me, like being with a woman. Like I said, they're magic."

—Kate, 29

Women are sensuous, seductive, erotic, and attractive. We are all powerful goddesses. It's been told over and over in history that we have the power to bring men to their knees and to make dynasties crumble. Feminine energy is one of the most powerful essences out there, and we all have the potential to be charmed by its beauty. And it's okay to be charmed. It's okay to fall under the spell of a woman. It might change your world, and it might not, but either way we could all use a little change.

Sexuality is fluid.

That is all you need to remember, and that is all you need to tell yourself if and when you have doubts. It ebbs and flows, waxes and wanes, and takes on many different forms over what might feel like many different lifetimes. Who we want to do today may not be who we want to do tomorrow, just as what we want to do with our life, our career, our investments—and even small things such as our hairstyle—will change again and again over time. It's only human nature.

It's these types of things that you need to remember when touching her smooth, soft, silky skin; when kissing her large, pink, hairless lips; when cupping her ripe, round breasts in your hands. You have a choice, and this is what you choose. And nobody can take that choice away from you. *Nobody.*

Not even those people who you fear might judge you—they are not a threat. You need to tell yourself that they have no right to judge you. And if you feel judged, you need to ask yourself why. Because maybe deep down the people judging you harbor some unexplored feelings or some unrequited love that they themselves can't explain. Maybe they are envious of you for being open to exploring new possibilities and experiences.

Don't take their words personally. It's not their life to live, it's yours. You have to make decisions that work for you. You have to take your own chances. Nobody can live your life for you, even those people who think they can.

There is no rhyme or reason to why we are attracted to certain people and not to others. There is no right or wrong reason to who it is we are attracted to. Those who aren't right for us treat us badly, abuse us or speak down to us, or make us feel uncomfortable all the time. But those who are right for us make us feel sexy, young, beautiful, and smart. It doesn't matter what their gender is; all that matters is that we enjoy them, they enjoy us, and they make us feel alive again. So enjoy whoever it is that you enjoy. Relish in the pleasure that they provide and bask in knowing that the choice is yours.

ON A LARGER SCALE

In the late 1940s, Alfred Kinsey published his own scale of sexuality based on people's fantasies and real-life experiences. The Kinsey Scale used a continuum model to show that people had the ability to have a range of flexibility in their sexual desires, preferences, and behaviors. On one end of the scale he placed a zero and on the other end, a six. A zero is a person who never even thought about a member of the same sex, and therefore would be considered a true heterosexual. A six is a person who has never thought about the opposite sex, and is therefore considered a true homosexual. The percentage of people falling into one of those categories is extremely low—less than 10 percent of the population. Between the zeros and the sixes, all of the numbers represent the varying degrees of same-sex/opposite-sex attraction. A three is a true bisexual.

Years later, Dr. Fritz Klein would go on to expand on the Kinsey model. Based on the idea that people's sexuality changed over the course of their lifetimes, Dr. Klein discussed the different factors that could influence identity. These are sexual attraction (to whom are you attracted?), sexual behavior (with whom do you actually have sex?), sexual fantasies (about whom do you fantasize?), emotional preference (do you love or like members of the same, opposite, or both sexes?), and social preference (with which sex do you socialize more often?). Dr. Klein wanted to show that sexuality did not involve merely whom we fantasized about and whom we screwed, but it also included our everyday interactions with our closest friends, and it was something that would evolve over time.

" I was always attracted to men, until I met Kate. She wasn't like any other woman I had ever met. So confident and intelligent, and when her arm brushed up against mine that very first time, I knew this was different . . ."

—Julia, 33

WOMEN ARE BEAUTIFUL

Women are beautiful—clearly and simply. It's ironic that in most of the animal kingdom, it's the men with the exquisite plumage or lavish adornments, but in the human world, it's women's curves, cuts, and styles that get the most attention.

TIP: Stand in front of the mirror and take the time to appreciate your own topography. What is it about yourself that you find most attractive?

There are many different types of women out there. Femme women are women who look and act ultrafeminine. They may wear only skirts or dresses to accentuate their curves. They generally have longer hair and wear makeup and jewelry. Butch women dress and act more masculine, wearing pants and button-downs. They often have short hair and the mannerisms of a confident guy. Of course, these are all generalizations, and there is a whole spectrum of women waiting to meet a woman like you.

Whether you decide to like your women pretty or handsome, deciding to like a woman is a bold and beautiful adventure. It's going to present you with delights and challenges that you can't possibly imagine. It's going to bring out your most passionate desires, and it will teach you a thing or two about who you are. There's no reason that you should come out of this experience feeling bad about yourself, especially since you are learning all the time about who you are, and this is a part of the process.

You can still be with men, or with men and women, or you can decide that love doesn't have a gender and fall for whoever makes you hot. It's all a decision that you will make, and remake, as you continue through life. And that's the beautiful thing about living; you get to make choices. And remake choices. So enjoy what you choose.

"I was definitely afraid the first time I was with a woman. Saying otherwise would be a lie. I wasn't sure I was ready for the experience, or what it might do to me. But once it began, I let go of all those thoughts and enjoyed it for what it was. It was a beautiful moment. And now, when I meet a woman I want, I don't sweat it. I just go for it, and let it be what it is."

—Jamie, 31

9

OH THE PLACES
YOU'LL GO

PLACES TO MEET

The journey into the Sapphic universe is full of wonder, delight, and information. If on your journey you decide to call on some extra help, there are a number of available resources at your command. Help might come in the form of a toy, a book, or a video, but wherever you find help, just know there's plenty of it available.

If you're looking to find a woman with whom to experiment, or even date, most online sites offer the option of meeting other women. You may meet the woman of your dreams on a dating site such as www.nerve.com. Or perhaps you'll place an ad on www.craigslist.org. Of course, you could also try www.myspace.com, www.tribe.net, or www.friendster.com. You never know whom you might meet, either through a friend or just through social networking. If it's only sex that you're looking for, you could check out a site such as www.adultfriendfinder.com.

COME TO SHOP OR SHOP TO COME

If you're looking for toys, you can always find a sex shop in your local neighborhood, but not all of them are going to be about giving you a quality experience. If you're looking for a place with a little more class, look for a sex positive store in your neighborhood, or try shopping online.

The nice thing about being able to physically shop for sex toys in stores is that they allow you to touch, but not try, the products before you buy them. Of course, nowadays, most online shops will give you thorough reviews of each toy, so you may be just as informed there when it comes to decision-making time. Either way, you should be able to find something you want or something you want to share with her or him.

Some sex-positive stores are:

www.adameve.com (Adam & Eve)

www.babeland.com (Babeland)

www.blowfish.com (Blowfish)

www.comeasyouare.com (Come As You Are)

www.evesgarden.com (Eve's Garden)

www.freddyandeddy.com (Freddy and Eddy)

www.goodvibes.com (Good Vibrations)

www.hiddenself.com (Hidden Self)

www.libida.com (Libida)

www.mypleasure.com (My Pleasure)

www.purplepassion.com (Purple Passion)

www.sheerglydedams.com (Glyde Dams)

www.smittenkittenonline.com (Smitten Kitten)

www.stockroom.com (JT's Stockroom)

VIDEOS

There are lots of videos out there, so instead of naming off a list of them, here are some words of advice. If you want to know anything about your vulva, check out one of Betty Dodson's videos—www.bettydodson.com. You might want to pick up her *Viva la Vulva: Women's Sex Organs Revealed.* If you're looking for more instructional videos, anything by Nina Hartley (www.adameve.com) should do the trick. I'd especially recommend *Nina Hartley's Guide to Making Love to Women* or *Nina Hartley's Guide to Strap-On Sex.* Also, *The Best of Vulva Massage* by Joseph Kramer, Ph.D., will give you a few additional tips on using your hands.

Of course, there's also erotica out there, which means, in this case, girl-on-girl porn. If you want to see hot lesbian scenes from the film world, check out www.clublez.com; and for a wide range of women-loving-women videos, visit www.fatalemedia.com. Pink and White Productions has also been getting great buzz, and its first two videos are *The Crash Pad* and *Superfreak,* available at blowfish.com. Maria Beatty's productions integrate kinky sex with beauty. Check out *The Black Glove* and *The Elegant Spanking.*

There are a million movies out there that you might enjoy. Erotic artist Andrew Blake's—www.andrewblake.com—girl/girl films are shot with style and class, and are cinematographically easy on the eyes. For a more thorough introduction to porn, check out Violet Blue's book *The Smart Girl's Guide to Porn.*

Any of the online stores will happily provide you with recommendations of videos you may want to watch. All it takes is a little bit of research. It's not that you need to have a video or a toy on hand for everyday use—though some women do like their vibrators or dildos—it's just that videos, toys, and other accoutrements are great devices to help enhance your relationships. You bring them into your sex life to help you titillate and tease both you and your partner. Plus, they can teach you about places you've never explored, and other places you'd like to go. They are there to help you explore what it is you like and discover new things you might want to try. Even if you don't add these things to your regular routine, it's nice to be able to have them on hand for a rainy day.

There's a whole world out there waiting for you to explore. So what are you waiting for?

FIVE RECOMMENDED
INSTRUCTIONAL VIDEOS

1. *Viva la Vulva: Women's Sex Organs Revealed* (Betty Dodson)

2. *Nina Hartley's Guide to Making Love to Women* (Adam & Eve)

3. *The Best of Vulva Massage* (Erospirit)

4. *Bend Over Boyfriend* (Fatale Media, Inc.)

5. *Female Ejaculation for Couples* (Fatale Media, Inc.)

ACKNOWLEDGMENTS

There's no rhyme or reason to the order of thanks, it's just the way it came out. Thanks to everyone who ever believed in me. Thanks to all the women who ever loved another woman. To Quiver for coming up with the idea. Thanks to my editor, Wendy, not only for helping me through the process but for reminding me to believe in myself. To Scott, for his continued interest in my work. Thanks to Candida Royalle not only for being the best mentor a girl could ask for but for also being a great friend. Thanks to all the other sex educators out there—those who came before me and those who will come after me—for your inspiration and your desire to make the world a safer place to have sex; and a special thank you to Barbara Carrellas for her insight and encouragement with this project. To Harry for telling me my words would appear in books someday. Thanks to the first girl I ever kissed for helping me discover my own sexual openness. To Amy, Leslie, and the rest of the goddesses for always putting up with me. Thanks to Konnie and Bill, Don and Brent, and everybody I met at Widener University for kicking me in the ass until I finished that master's. To Bob B. for getting me on the path. To *Playgirl* magazine, and Michele Zipp, for taking a chance on me. To Chaunce, for keeping it real. Thanks to everyone who shared their stories with me and who allowed me to graciously use their words as a contribution to this book. Thanks to Babeland—and especially Rachel Venning and Claire Cavanah—for five years of the best retail job ever. Thanks to Blue for keeping me company every day that I wrote this. Thanks to my family, and especially my parents, for supporting me no matter what. And a special thank you to my love, Jonny—for adding sparkle to my world by showing me love and support, even in my ugliest of hours.

ABOUT THE AUTHOR

Jamye Waxman has been called "the nexxxt generation of sex educator" (wired.com). With a master's degree in sexuality education from Widener University, and more than ten years of experience working in media, Jamye is one of the newest and loudest voices in the field of sexology. She currently writes three sex columns, including the sex-advice column "Sex Ed" for *Playgirl* magazine and dating and relationship columns for *Steppin' Out* magazine and *Philly Edge*. Jamye has contributed to *Naked Ambition: Women Who Are Changing Pornography* (Carroll & Graf, 2005), and *Women's Health* magazine. She is also the cowriter and producer of the latest Candida Royalle feature, *Under the Covers* (Femme Productions) and teaches classes on all things sex. In addition, she is the former radio producer of *LoveBytes* with Bob Berkowitz, *The Joan Rivers Show*, and *The Alan Colmes Show*, and the former host of *Aural Fixation*. She was a producer of the popular Metro TV show *Naked New York*. For five years, Jamye was a sex educator at the world-famous sex shop Babeland (formerly Toys in Babeland) in New York City. She is president of Feminists for Free Expression, www.ffeusa.org. She has her own Web site and blog at www.jamyewaxman.com.

OTHER HOT BOOKS FROM QUIVER

WET
Erotic Adventures in Water
By Ellen Kate
ISBN-13: 978-1-59233-257-1
ISBN-10: 1-59233-257-9
$19.99/£12.99/$25.95 CAN

WET submerges you into new depths of ecstasy. Featuring full-color, highly artistic and titillating photographs, shot on location in Los Cabos, Mexico, the book provides readers with suggestions for various aquatic venues and sex positions, aqueous foreplay and masturbation techniques, methods for simultaneous orgasms underwater, recommendations for water-friendly sex toys, as well as sexy games you can play in and under the water. Testimonials and anecdotes from people who have engaged in aquatic sex are also included. No matter what your particular situation, making love in the water can take you a step away from your typical love life and add some spontaneity and adventure to the mix. WET is an ideal book for honeymooners or people who treasure "vacation sex."

THE SEX BIBLE
The Complete Guide to Sexual Love
By Susan Crain Bakos
ISBN-13: 978-1-59233-227-4
ISBN-10: 1-59233-227-7
$30.00/£19.99/$38.95 CAN

The Sex Bible is an authoritative, comprehensive, and beautifully photographed sex resource book that provides in-depth treatment of sexual topics in frank detail. The book is arranged into different sections, including "Foreplay," "Sex Toys," and "Oral Sex." It explores sexual subjects you are either familiar with, or until now, never even knew existed. Couples will be captivated by personal anecdotes interspersed throughout. Illustrated with full-color photography, *The Sex Bible* will not only educate couples, but also it will help heighten sexual enjoyment.

THE ART OF THE QUICKIE
Fast Sex, Fast Orgasm, Anytime, Anywhere
By Joel D. Block, Ph.D.
ISBN-13: 978-1-59233-240-3
ISBN-10: 1-59233-240-4
$19.99/£12.99/$25.95 CAN

The Art of the Quickie will coach readers how to have quick, but rewarding sex. Quickies can be even more fulfilling as those long sessions because the thrill involved in having sex unexpectedly or in forbidden locations adds a potent element of excitement. But what about women, is the quickie fair to them? *The Art of the Quickie* features definitive guidelines for women to experience faster orgasms—in 5 minutes!—thereby relieving men of the performance anxiety that often accompanies the responsibility of bringing their partners to orgasm.

Visit our Web site at www.quiverbooks.com